THE BEATLES FOR TWO

Arrangements by Mark Phillips

Cover photo: CBS Photo Archive via Getty Images

ISBN 978-1-5400-4817-2

Visit Hal Leonard Online at
www.halleonard.com

Contact us:
Hal Leonard
7777 West Bluemound Road
Milwaukee, WI 53213
Email: info@halleonard.com

In Europe, contact:
Hal Leonard Europe Limited
42 Wigmore Street
Marylebone, London, W1U 2RN
Email: info@halleonardeurope.com

In Australia, contact:
Hal Leonard Australia Pty. Ltd.
4 Lentara Court
Cheltenham, Victoria, 3192 Australia
Email: info@halleonard.com.au

ALL MY LOVING

TROMBONES

Words and Music by JOHN LENNON
and PAUL McCARTNEY

ALL YOU NEED IS LOVE

TROMBONES

Words and Music by JOHN LENNON
and PAUL McCARTNEY

AND I LOVE HER

TROMBONES

Words and Music by JOHN LENNON
and PAUL McCARTNEY

ELEANOR RIGBY

TROMBONES

Words and Music by JOHN LENNON
and PAUL McCARTNEY

Moderately fast

THE FOOL ON THE HILL

TROMBONES

Words and Music by JOHN LENNON
and PAUL McCARTNEY

Moderately slow, in 2

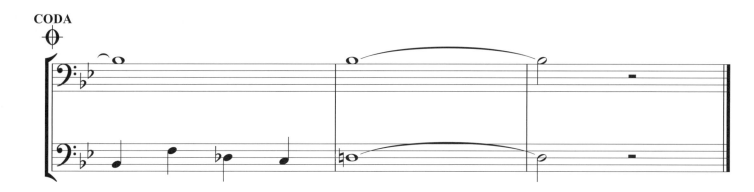

GOLDEN SLUMBERS

TROMBONES

Words and Music by JOHN LENNON
and PAUL McCARTNEY

HERE COMES THE SUN

TROMBONES

Words and Music by
GEORGE HARRISON

Moderately fast

HERE, THERE AND EVERYWHERE

TROMBONES

Words and Music by JOHN LENNON
and PAUL McCARTNEY

HEY JUDE

TROMBONES

Words and Music by JOHN LENNON
and PAUL McCARTNEY

I SAW HER STANDING THERE

TROMBONES

Words and Music by JOHN LENNON
and PAUL McCARTNEY

D.S. al Coda
(no repeat)

CODA

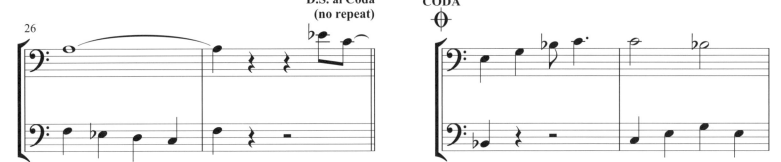

I WANT TO HOLD YOUR HAND

TROMBONES

Words and Music by JOHN LENNON
and PAUL McCARTNEY

Moderately fast

I WILL

TROMBONES

Words and Music by JOHN LENNON
and PAUL McCARTNEY

LET IT BE

TROMBONES

Words and Music by JOHN LENNON
and PAUL McCARTNEY

THE LONG AND WINDING ROAD

TROMBONES

Words and Music by JOHN LENNON
and PAUL McCARTNEY

MICHELLE

TROMBONES

Words and Music by JOHN LENNON
and PAUL McCARTNEY

Moderately slow, in 2

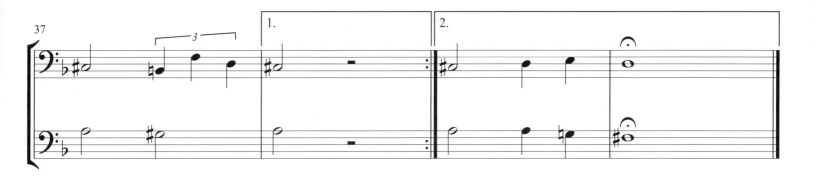

NORWEGIAN WOOD
(This Bird Has Flown)

TROMBONES

Words and Music by JOHN LENNON
and PAUL McCARTNEY

OB-LA-DI, OB-LA-DA

TROMBONES

Words and Music by JOHN LENNON
and PAUL McCARTNEY

Brightly, in 2

PENNY LANE

TROMBONES

Words and Music by JOHN LENNON
and PAUL McCARTNEY

Moderately

SHE LOVES YOU

TROMBONES

Words and Music by JOHN LENNON
and PAUL McCARTNEY

Moderately fast

SOMETHING

TROMBONES

Words and Music by
GEORGE HARRISON

WHEN I'M SIXTY-FOUR

TROMBONES

Words and Music by JOHN LENNON
and PAUL McCARTNEY

YELLOW SUBMARINE

TROMBONES

Words and Music by JOHN LENNON
and PAUL McCARTNEY

YESTERDAY

TROMBONES

Words and Music by JOHN LENNON
and PAUL McCARTNEY